MEASURES *of* SUCCESS®

A Comprehensive Musicianship Band Method

DEBORAH A. SHELDON • BRIAN BALMAGES • TIMOTHY LOEST • ROBERT SHELDON

PERCUSSION WRITTEN AND EDITED BY DAVID COLLIER

Welcome to *Measures of Success* and the amazing world of instrumental music! You are about to begin an exciting musical journey full of rewards and challenges. As you practice, you will find yourself sharing the gift of music with family, friends, and audiences. So get ready—your path to success begins now!

HISTORY OF THE OBOE

The oboe is a member of the woodwind family. It is referred to as a "double reed" instrument because its reed consists of two pieces of cane fastened together around a small metal tube. When played, the two reeds vibrate against each other to create the sound. The invention of the oboe is usually credited to French musicians Jean Hotteterre and Michel Philidor. An instrument that predates the oboe from the 1100s is called the shawm. The shawm was modified over many years, eventually leading to the development of the oboe in the 1600s. While the shawm was made from one continuous piece of wood, the oboe was designed to have three sections that fit together. The word oboe comes from the French word "hautbois" which means "high wood." By the 1700s, the oboe was a common instrument in the orchestra. Today it is a prominent member of both bands and orchestras.

ABOUT THIS BOOK

The first 14 pages of your book are divided into A and B pages. The A pages put you in a special register that is for your instrument only. The B pages let you play along with the rest of the band. Page 14c will help get all oboe players familiar with the same notes before proceeding further.

Production: Frank J. Hackinson
Production Coordinators: Ken Mattis, Brian Balmages, and Philip Groeber
Cover Design and Interior Line Drawings: Danielle Taylor and Adrianne Hirosky
Interior Layout and Design: Andi Whitmer
Engraving: Tempo Music Press, Inc.
Printer: Tempo Music Press, Inc.

ISBN-13: 978-1-56939-804-3

THE FJH MUSIC COMPANY INC.

Frank J. Hackinson

OBOE ASSEMBLY

UPPER JOINT

SIDE OCTAVE KEY

KEYS

BACK OCTAVE KEY

HALF HOLE

CORK

KEYS

LOWER JOINT

CORK

BELL

Photograph courtesy of Yamaha Corporation of America

STEP 1

Lay your case flat on the floor. Open your case right side up.

STEP 2

Apply a thin coat of cork grease to each cork if needed. Occasionally wipe off old cork grease to prevent buildup. Be sure to clean your hands.

STEP 3

Using the reed soaker cup, immerse the tip of the reed in a 1/2-inch of water. Soak the reed long enough for the tip to be pliable. Avoid over-soaking the reed.

STEP 4

Pick up the bell with your right hand. If your oboe has a bell key, press it closed with your right thumb. Pick up the lower joint with you left hand, palm below the thumb rest. Gently twist the bell onto the lower joint.

STEP 5

Transfer the lower section to your right hand, holding it away from the keys. Pick up the upper joint with your left hand keeping the bridge keys raised. With the upper and lower bridge keys aligned, gently twist the two sections together.

STEP 6

Take reed from soaker cup, remove excess moisture, and insert its cork end into the oboe using a gentle twisting motion.

CHECK IT OUT!

POSTURE CHECKLIST
- Sit on the front edge of the chair
- Feet flat on the floor
- Sit straight and tall
- Shoulders relaxed
- Elbows comfortably away from your sides

HAND POSITION CHECKLIST
- Right thumb is under the thumb rest
- Left thumb is positioned to control octave key on back of oboe
- Fingers are curved naturally
- Pads of fingertips are ready to depress tone hole keys

EMBOUCHURE CHECKLIST
- Reed is placed on the center of the lower lip
- Lips close naturally, rolling the reed inward
- Lips cushion the reed with equal pressure on all sides
- Embouchure relaxed, throat open

OBOE SUPPLIES

- reeds
- reed case
- thin oboe swab
- cork grease
- soft cloth

OBOE CARE

DAILY
- Remove reed, allow it to dry, and place it into the reed case
- Swab out all sections
- Wipe away moisture from tenon openings with soft cloth
- Wipe away fingerprints with soft cloth

WEEKLY
- Grease tenon corks (wipe away old cork grease to prevent buildup)

MONTHLY
- Inspect for loose pads, rods, springs, and missing corks

YEARLY
- Take your oboe to an authorized repair shop for a tune-up

NEVER
- Never submerge your oboe in water
- Never apply cleaners or polishes to your oboe
- Never adjust or oil your oboe keys – leave this for a repair shop
- Never leave your oboe unattended, or on the floor or chair
- Never keep anything in your case except for your instrument, reeds, and care supplies

PRELUDE: SOUNDS BEFORE SYMBOLS

BREATHING

The key to playing a wind instrument well begins with taking a good breath. With just your reed, take a full, relaxed breath and play a steady tone. How long can you hold it?

PITCH, BEAT, AND RHYTHM

Pitch is the highness or lowness of a note or tone. The **beat** is the pulse of the music.
Rhythm is a pattern of short or long sounds (or silences) that fit with a steady beat.

ARTICULATION

Articulation is how the tongue and the air begin a note. Your director will show you how to articulate a note.

With just your reed, play some of the familiar songs below. Since you are only using your reed, the *pitch* will stay the same, while the *rhythm* will identify the song. Articulate clearly!

Bingo	**Jingle Bells**	**London Bridge**
Mary Had a Little Lamb	**Old MacDonald**	**Twinkle, Twinkle Little Star**

MAKING MUSIC

With your director's help, assemble your entire oboe carefully. You are now ready for your first three notes!

Hold each note with a good sound until you are comfortable with it. Next, articulate each note four times and then rest for four beats. Remember to focus on posture, hand position, and tone quality.

AND WE'RE OFF!

(hold)   (rest)
A ———→ | − − − − | A A A A | − − − − | (repeat this with your other two new notes)
1 2 3 4   1 2 3 4   1 2 3 4   1 2 3 4

AU CLAIRE DE LA LUNE

F F F G | A − G − | F A G G | F ──→ − − |
1 2 3 4   1 2 3 4   1 2 3 4   1 2 3 4

HOT CROSS BUNS

A ──→ G ──→ | F ──→ − − | A ──→ G ──→ | F ──→ − − | F F F F | G G G G | A ──→ G ──→ | F ──→ − − |
1 2 3 4   1 2 3 4   1 2 3 4   1 2 3 4   1 2 3 4   1 2 3 4   1 2 3 4   1 2 3 4

MARY HAD A LITTLE LAMB

A G F G | A A A − | G G G − | A A A − | A G F G | A A A − | G G A G | F ──→ − − |
1 2 3 4   1 2 3 4   1 2 3 4   1 2 3 4   1 2 3 4   1 2 3 4   1 2 3 4   1 2 3 4

COMPOSER'S CORNER

It is your turn to compose your *own* piece of music! Use the three notes you know to complete this piece. Give it a title and perform it for a friend or family member!

Title:_____   Composer (your name):_____

F __ __ __ | __ − __ − | __ __ __ − | __ __ F − |

PRELUDE: SOUNDS BEFORE SYMBOLS

BREATHING

The key to playing a wind instrument well begins with taking a good breath. With just your reed,
take a full, relaxed breath and play a steady tone. How long can you hold it?

PITCH, BEAT, AND RHYTHM

Pitch is the highness or lowness of a note or tone. The **beat** is the pulse of the music.
Rhythm is a pattern of short or long sounds (or silences) that fit with a steady beat.

ARTICULATION

Articulation is how the tongue and the air begin a note. Your director will show you how to articulate a note.

With just your reed, play some of the familiar songs below. Since you are only using your reed,
the *pitch* will stay the same, while the *rhythm* will identify the song. Articulate clearly!

Bingo	**Jingle Bells**	**London Bridge**
Mary Had a Little Lamb	**Old MacDonald**	**Twinkle, Twinkle Little Star**

MAKING MUSIC

With your director's help, assemble your entire oboe carefully. You are now ready for your first three notes!

NEW NOTE! D **NEW NOTE! C** **NEW NOTE! Bb**

Hold each note with a good sound until you are comfortable with it. Next, articulate each note four times and then rest for four beats.
Remember to focus on posture, hand position, and tone quality.

AND WE'RE OFF!

(hold)   (rest)

D——→ | – – – – | D D D D | – – – – | (repeat this with your other two new notes)

1 2 3 4   1 2 3 4   1 2 3 4   1 2 3 4

AU CLAIRE DE LA LUNE

Bb Bb Bb C | D – C – | Bb D C C | Bb——→ – – |

1 2 3 4   1 2 3 4   1 2 3 4   1 2 3 4

HOT CROSS BUNS

D —→ C —→ | Bb —→ – – | D —→ C —→ | Bb —→ – – | Bb Bb Bb Bb | C C C C | D —→ C —→ | Bb —→ – – |

1 2 3 4   1 2 3 4   1 2 3 4   1 2 3 4   1 2 3 4   1 2 3 4   1 2 3 4   1 2 3 4

MARY HAD A LITTLE LAMB

D C Bb C | D D D – | C C C – | D D D – | D C Bb C | D D D – | C C D C | Bb —→ – – |

1 2 3 4   1 2 3 4   1 2 3 4   1 2 3 4   1 2 3 4   1 2 3 4   1 2 3 4   1 2 3 4

COMPOSER'S CORNER

It is your turn to compose your *own* piece of music! Use the three notes you know to complete this piece.
Give it a title and perform it for a friend or family member!

Title:_____   Composer (your name):_____

Bb __ __ __ __ | —→ – __ – | __ __ __ __ – | __ __ Bb – |

OPUS 1

THEORY

MUSIC STAFF
The **music staff** is where notes and rests are written. It has 5 lines and 4 spaces.

LONG TONE
A **long tone** is a held note. The fermata ($\frown$) indicates to hold the note until your teacher tells you to rest.

BAR LINES
Bar lines divide the music staff into measures.

FINAL BAR LINE
A **final bar** line indicates the end of a piece.

1.1 FIRST NOTE *Practice each long tone daily to improve your sound!*

Accompaniments for all A pages can be downloaded at www.fjhmusic.com/mos

NEW NOTE!
A

final bar line →

RHYTHM

BEAT
The **beat** is the pulse of the music. Tap your foot to keep a steady beat!

NOTES AND RESTS
Notes represent sound. **Rests** represent silence.

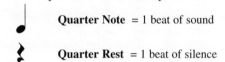

♩ **Quarter Note** = 1 beat of sound

𝄽 **Quarter Rest** = 1 beat of silence

1.2 FOUR IN A ROW *This piece has four beats in each measure. Remember to tap your foot.*

1.3 SECOND NOTE

NEW NOTE!
G

1.4 FOUR MORE *How many measures do you see?*

1.5 UP AND DOWN *Any time you see a Bonus Box, write in the note name.*

BONUS BOX

1.6 ALL MIXED UP

BONUS BOX

OPUS 1

MUSIC STAFF

The **music staff** is where notes and rests are written. It has 5 lines and 4 spaces.

LONG TONE

A **long tone** is a held note. The fermata (⌢) indicates to hold the note until your teacher tells you to rest.

measures

BAR LINES

Bar lines divide the music staff into measures.

FINAL BAR LINE

A **final bar** line indicates the end of a piece.

1.1 FIRST NOTE *Practice each long tone daily to improve your sound!*

NEW NOTE! D

final bar line

RHYTHM

BEAT

The **beat** is the pulse of the music. Tap your foot to keep a steady beat!

1 2 3 4

NOTES AND RESTS

Notes represent sound. **Rests** represent silence.

Quarter Note = 1 beat of sound

Quarter Rest = 1 beat of silence

1.2 FOUR IN A ROW *This piece has four beats in each measure. Remember to tap your foot.*

1.3 SECOND NOTE

NEW NOTE! C

1.4 FOUR MORE *How many measures do you see?*

1.5 UP AND DOWN *Any time you see a Bonus Box, write in the note name.*

BONUS BOX

1.6 ALL MIXED UP

BONUS BOX

BB208OB

ACCIDENTALS

Accidentals are signs that alter a note's pitch. They are placed to the left of the note.

Flat (♭) A flat sign lowers the pitch by one half-step. This pitch remains lowered for the rest of the measure.

Sharp (♯) A sharp sign raises the pitch by one half-step. This pitch remains raised for the rest of the measure.

Natural (♮) A natural sign cancels a flat or sharp. It remains cancelled for the rest of the measure.

1.7 THIRD NOTE'S A CHARM

1.8 ALL TOGETHER

1.9 WHAT GOES UP...

1.10 RHYTHM RENDEZVOUS

CLEFS

Clefs are signs that help name notes.

The **treble clef**, also called the **G clef**, names G on the treble staff. The inside tail wraps around 2nd line G. The musical alphabet uses A B C D E F and G. Each line and space of the staff has a note name. To find a treble clef note, move up or down by lines and spaces in the musical alphabet sequence.

D E F G A B C D E F G

LEDGER LINES

Ledger lines extend the staff. Notes written above or below the staff appear with ledger lines.

NAME THAT NOTE... *Use your knowledge of the musical alphabet to fill in the Bonus Boxes!*

A B C D ☐ F ☐ A ☐ ☐ D E ☐ G ☐ B ☐ ☐

ACCIDENTALS

Accidentals are signs that alter a note's pitch. They are placed to the left of the note.

Flat (♭) A flat sign lowers the pitch by one half-step. This pitch remains lowered for the rest of the measure.

Sharp (♯) A sharp sign raises the pitch by one half-step. This pitch remains raised for the rest of the measure.

Natural (♮) A natural sign cancels a flat or sharp. It remains cancelled for the rest of the measure.

1.7 THIRD NOTE'S A CHARM

1.8 ALL TOGETHER

1.9 WHAT GOES UP...

1.10 RHYTHM RENDEZVOUS

CLEFS

Clefs are signs that help name notes.

The **treble clef**, also called the **G clef**, names G on the treble staff. The inside tail wraps around 2nd line G. The musical alphabet uses A B C D E F and G. Each line and space of the staff has a note name. To find a treble clef note, move up or down by lines and spaces in the musical alphabet sequence.

D E F G A B C D E F G

LEDGER LINES

Ledger lines extend the staff. Notes written above or below the staff appear with ledger lines.

NAME THAT NOTE... *Use your knowledge of the musical alphabet to fill in the Bonus Boxes!*

A B C D ☐ F ☐ A ☐ ☐ D E ☐ G ☐ B ☐

BB208OB

HALF NOTES AND WHOLE NOTES

Half Note
2 beats of sound

Whole Note
4 beats of sound

HALF RESTS AND WHOLE RESTS

Half Rest
2 beats of silence
(sits on a line)

Whole Rest
4 beats of silence
(hangs from a line)

TIME SIGNATURE

The top number shows the number of beats in each measure.
The bottom number shows the type of note that receives one beat.
*Hint: Replace the top number with a "1" and you will get a
fraction that equals the type of note that gets one beat!*

Number of beats in a measure
Type of note that gets one beat

1.11 GOING PLACES *Circle the half rests.*

FERMATA

When playing on your own, hold a note with a
fermata longer than its assigned value.

1.12 COUNTDOWN *Hold the note with a fermata longer than its assigned value.*

REPEAT SIGN

A **repeat sign** is a final bar line with two dots.
Without stopping, go back to the beginning
and play the music a second time.

1.13 TURN AROUND *Say the note names and demonstrate your fingerings before you play.*

1.14 HOT CROSS BUNS

English Folk Song

1.15 HERE WE GO! *Draw in the bar lines, then play!*

RHYTHM

HALF NOTES AND WHOLE NOTES

Half Note
2 beats of sound

Whole Note
4 beats of sound

HALF RESTS AND WHOLE RESTS

Half Rest
2 beats of silence
(sits on a line)

Whole Rest
4 beats of silence
(hangs from a line)

TIME SIGNATURE

The top number shows the number of beats in each measure.
The bottom number shows the type of note that receives one beat.
Hint: Replace the top number with a "1" and you will get a fraction that equals the type of note that gets one beat!

Number of beats in a measure
Type of note that gets one beat

1.11 GOING PLACES *Circle the half rests.*

time signature

TRACK 1 12

THEORY

FERMATA

When playing on your own, hold a note with a **fermata** longer than its assigned value.

1.12 COUNTDOWN *Hold the note with a fermata longer than its assigned value.*

fermata

TRACK 1 13

THEORY

REPEAT SIGN

A **repeat sign** is a final bar line with two dots. Without stopping, go back to the beginning and play the music a second time.

1.13 TURN AROUND *Say the note names and demonstrate your fingerings before you play.*

TRACK 1 14

repeat sign

1.14 HOT CROSS BUNS

English Folk Song

TRACK 1 15

1.15 HERE WE GO! *Draw in the bar lines, then play!*

BONUS BOX

TRACK 1 16

BB208OB

1.16 AU CLAIRE DE LA LUNE *Musicianship Challenge! – Without the accompaniment,*
play 1ˢᵗ time quietly, 2ⁿᵈ time loudly.

French Folk Song

1.17 MARY HAD A LITTLE LAMB

Traditional

1.18 MARY HAD A COOL LAMB

Traditional Melody

STYLE AND FORM: DUET

A **duet** has two different parts performed simultaneously by two individuals or groups.

1.19 BEAT STREET — Duet *A Beat Street exercise indicates to clap the rhythm.*

1.20 DUET LIKE THIS

1.21 CLIMBING HIGHER

1.22 HOME BASE

1.23 EVEN HIGHER! *Trace the clef!*

THEORY

PHRASING

A **phrase** in music is similar to a sentence in speech. It should continue uninterrupted until the music indicates a breath.

♪ A **breath mark** indicates to take a breath through your mouth.

1.24 DOWN BY THE STATION

American Folk Song

breath mark →

HISTORY

MUSIC

Stephen Collins Foster (1826 – 1864) was an American songwriter born in Pennsylvania. He published his first piece when he was 18 years old. Some of his most famous songs are *Oh! Susanna, Camptown Races,* and *Some Folks Do.* His compositions capture the spirit of American folk music during the 1800s.

ART

During this time in history, artists of the Hudson River School were hard at work in the United States. Frederic Church painted *Morning, Looking East Over the Hudson Valley from the Catskill Mountains* about the same time that *Camptown Races* was written.

WORLD

The world was introduced to Ebenezer Scrooge (the famous character in Charles Dickens' *A Christmas Carol*), Abraham Lincoln delivered the Gettysburg Address, and the stapler was patented.

1.25 SOME FOLKS DO

 Before you play, draw these symbols where they belong: Treble Clef, Time Signature, Final Bar Line.

Stephen C. Foster

1.26 SCALING THE WALL *Work with another student to learn this piece.*

BONUS BOX

ON THE PODIUM

CONDUCTING IN 4/4 TIME

Your band director has been conducting a four-beat pattern. Now it is your turn to conduct! Place your right hand in a "handshake" position and follow the diagram to conduct in 4/4 time.

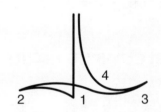

1.27 GOOD KING WENCESLAS *Conduct a partner, your section, or the entire class!*

ON THE PODIUM

English Carol

1.28 STOMP ROCK

stomp

9b

THEORY

PHRASING

A **phrase** in music is similar to a sentence in speech. It should continue uninterrupted until the music indicates a breath.

, A **breath mark** indicates to take a breath through your mouth.

1.24 DOWN BY THE STATION

American Folk Song

breath mark→

HISTORY

MUSIC
Stephen Collins Foster (1826 – 1864) was an American songwriter born in Pennsylvania. He published his first piece when he was 18 years old. Some of his most famous songs are *Oh! Susanna*, *Camptown Races*, and *Some Folks Do*. His compositions capture the spirit of American folk music during the 1800s.

ART
During this time in history, artists of the Hudson River School were hard at work in the United States. Frederic Church painted *Morning, Looking East Over the Hudson Valley from the Catskill Mountains* about the same time that *Camptown Races* was written.

WORLD
The world was introduced to Ebenezer Scrooge (the famous character in Charles Dickens' *A Christmas Carol*), Abraham Lincoln delivered the Gettysburg Address, and the stapler was patented.

1.25 SOME FOLKS DO *Before you play, draw these symbols where they belong: Treble Clef, Time Signature, Final Bar Line.*

Stephen C. Foster

1.26 SCALING THE WALL *Work with another student to learn this piece.*

BONUS BOX

ON THE PODIUM

CONDUCTING IN 4/4 TIME

Your band director has been conducting a four-beat pattern. Now it is your turn to conduct! Place your right hand in a "handshake" position and follow the diagram to conduct in 4/4 time.

1.27 GOOD KING WENCESLAS *Conduct a partner, your section, or the entire class!*

English Carol

ON THE PODIUM

1.28 STOMP ROCK

stomp

BB208OB

OPUS 1 ENCORE!

INTERPRETATION STATION

Listen to CD 1 Track 30. Describe the music and how it makes you feel.

SIMON "SEZ"

Your director will give you a starting note. Listen to the rhythms your director plays and echo them back. Listen carefully!

COMPOSER'S CORNER

A composer is someone who creates original music. It is YOUR turn to be a composer!
Using the notes you already know, complete this composition. Guide rhythms have been provided for you in parentheses.

Title:_____ Name:_____

PENCIL POWER

Match the following terms with their symbols.

1. _____ Clef	6. _____ Quarter Note	A: B: C: D:
2. _____ Time Signature	7. _____ Whole Note	
3. _____ Repeat Sign	8. _____ Whole Rest	E: F: G: H:
4. _____ Fermata	9. _____ Half Rest	
5. _____ Half Note	10. _____ Quarter Rest	I: J:

CURTAIN UP!

Time to perform! Practice these pieces and play them for friends or family members. Introduce each piece by its title.
Remember to bow when you are finished!

1.29 GO TELL AUNT RHODY *Teach your audience to conduct a four-beat pattern!*

American Folk Song

1.30 CUCKOO SAMBA

1.31 LIGHTLY ROW — Duet *Pair up with a friend to perform this piece for your audience. Switch parts on the repeat!*

Traditional

OPUS 1 ENCORE!

INTERPRETATION STATION

TRACK 1 30

Listen to CD 1 Track 30. Describe the music and how it makes you feel.

SIMON "SEZ"

Your director will give you a starting note. Listen to the rhythms your director plays and echo them back. Listen carefully!

COMPOSER'S CORNER

A composer is someone who creates original music. It is YOUR turn to be a composer!
Using the notes you already know, complete this composition. Guide rhythms have been provided for you in parentheses.

Title:_____   Name:_____

PENCIL POWER

Match the following terms with their symbols.

1. _____ Clef   6. _____ Quarter Note

2. _____ Time Signature   7. _____ Whole Note

3. _____ Repeat Sign   8. _____ Whole Rest

4. _____ Fermata   9. _____ Half Rest

5. _____ Half Note   10. _____ Quarter Rest

A: 𝄇   B: 𝄽   C: 𝄴   D: ▬

E: 𝅝   F: ▬   G: 𝄐   H: 𝅗𝅥

I: 𝄞   J: ♩

CURTAIN UP!

Time to perform! Practice these pieces and play them for friends or family members. Introduce each piece by its title.
Remember to bow when you are finished!

1.29 GO TELL AUNT RHODY *Teach your audience to conduct a four-beat pattern!*

American Folk Song

TRACK 1 31

ON THE PODIUM

1.30 CUCKOO SAMBA

TRACK 1 32

1.31 LIGHTLY ROW — Duet *Pair up with a friend to perform this piece for your audience. Switch parts on the repeat!*

Traditional

TRACK 1 33

BB208OB

OPUS 2

HISTORY

MUSIC

Ludwig van Beethoven (1770 – 1827) lived most of his life in Vienna, Austria. His music became a bridge between Classical and Romantic music. When *Symphony No. 9* and its *Ode to Joy* were performed for the first time, Beethoven was completely deaf!

ART

Romanticism in art was an important movement in Europe and themes often included nationalism. Eugene Delacroix was one of the most important French artists. His *Liberty Leading the People* commemorates the French Revolution of 1830 and the overthrow of King Charles X.

WORLD

Around this time in history, Mexico became a republic, trains first carried passengers in England, the first photograph was taken, and ice cream was first sold in the United States!

2.1 ODE TO JOY *Musicianship Challenge! – Without the accompaniment, play the 1ˢᵗ phrase gently, the 2ⁿᵈ phrase majestically.*

Ludwig van Beethoven

2.2 OUTER LIMITS

NEW NOTE! **D**

2.3 OLD MACDONALD

American Folk Song
continue to the next line

2.4 SHARK! *Musicianship Challenge! – Without the accompaniment, play this like you are being chased.*

NEW NOTE! **E**

Choose any note you have learned!

2.5 CRUSADER'S HYMN *Play each phrase in one breath.*

Silesian Folk Song

THEORY

KEY SIGNATURE

The **key signature** indicates which notes to play sharp or flat. It appears at the beginning of each staff.

- There can be up to 7 sharps in a key signature. **Sharps** (♯) follow this order: F, C, G, D, A, E, B
- There can be up to 7 flats in a key signature. **Flats** (♭) follow this order: B, E, A, D, G, C, F
- Your key signature in 2.6, *Keynote March*, indicates that all Bs should be played as B-flats

This is the key of **F Major**.

2.6 KEYNOTE MARCH *Musicianship Challenge! – Play this piece like you would hear it in a parade.*

key signature

OPUS 2

MUSIC

Ludwig van Beethoven (1770 – 1827) lived most of his life in Vienna, Austria. His music became a bridge between Classical and Romantic music. When *Symphony No. 9* and its *Ode to Joy* were performed for the first time, Beethoven was completely deaf!

ART

Romanticism in art was an important movement in Europe and themes often included nationalism. Eugene Delacroix was one of the most important French artists. His *Liberty Leading the People* commemorates the French Revolution of 1830 and the overthrow of King Charles X.

WORLD

Around this time in history, Mexico became a republic, trains first carried passengers in England, the first photograph was taken, and ice cream was first sold in the United States!

2.1 ODE TO JOY *Musicianship Challenge! – Without the accompaniment, play the 1ˢᵗ phrase gently, the 2ⁿᵈ phrase majestically.* Ludwig van Beethoven

2.2 OUTER LIMITS

2.3 OLD MACDONALD American Folk Song

continue to the next line

2.4 SHARK! *Musicianship Challenge! – Without the CD, play this like you are being chased.*

Choose any note you have learned!

2.5 CRUSADER'S HYMN *Play each phrase in one breath.* Silesian Folk Song

KEY SIGNATURE

The **key signature** indicates which notes to play sharp or flat. It appears at the beginning of each staff.

- There can be up to 7 sharps in a key signature. **Sharps** (♯) follow this order: F, C, G, D, A, E, B
- There can be up to 7 flats in a key signature. **Flats** (♭) follow this order: B, E, A, D, G, C, F
- Your key signature in 2.6, *Keynote March,* indicates that all Bs and Es should be played as B-flats and E-flats.

This is the key of B♭ Major.

2.6 KEYNOTE MARCH *Musicianship Challenge! – Play this piece like you would hear it in a parade.*

12a

HISTORY

MUSIC

Wolfgang Amadeus Mozart (1756 – 1791) was born in Salzburg, Austria. He was a child genius and composed his first minuet when he was just five years old! During his short life of 35 years, he wrote over 600 musical compositions. Many of his works continue to be performed today.

ART

As Mozart wrote in the Classical style, Neoclassicism in visual art was being explored by artists such as Jacques-Louis David, a French painter. This style can be seen in his painting, *The Death of Socrates,* which was completed in 1787.

WORLD

The thirteen American Colonies broke away from the British Empire in the American Revolutionary War, the *Declaration of Independence* was signed, and Johnny Appleseed was born.

2.7 STAR SEARCH *This piece is in the key of _____ Major.*

French Melody
adapted by Wolfgang A. Mozart

THEORY

DYNAMICS

Dynamics indicate how loudly or softly to play. Italian terms are often used in music to indicate volume.

p (*piano*) – play softly   *f* (*forte*) – play loudly

2.8 BEAT STREET *Clap the rhythm with dynamics!*

CLAP

2.9 LONDON BRIDGE *Show phrasing by placing breath marks in this piece before you play it.*

English Folk Song

2.10 JINGLE BELLS – Duet

James S. Pierpont

BB208OB

12b

HISTORY

MUSIC

Wolfgang Amadeus Mozart (1756 – 1791) was born in Salzburg, Austria. He was a child genius and composed his first minuet when he was just five years old! During his short life of 35 years, he wrote over 600 musical compositions. Many of his works continue to be performed today.

ART

As Mozart wrote in the Classical style, Neoclassicism in visual art was being explored by artists such as Jacques-Louis David, a French painter. This style can be seen in his painting, *The Death of Socrates,* which was completed in 1787.

WORLD

The thirteen American Colonies broke away from the British Empire in the American Revolutionary War, the *Declaration of Independence* was signed, and Johnny Appleseed was born.

2.7 STAR SEARCH *This piece is in the key of _____ Major.*

French Melody
adapted by Wolfgang A. Mozart

TRACK 1 • 40

THEORY

DYNAMICS

Dynamics indicate how loudly or softly to play. Italian terms are often used in music to indicate volume.

$\boldsymbol{p}$ (*piano*) – play softly $\boldsymbol{f}$ (*forte*) – play loudly

---

2.8 BEAT STREET *Clap the rhythm with dynamics!*

TRACK 1 • 41

CLAP

2.9 LONDON BRIDGE *Show phrasing by placing breath marks in this piece before you play it.*

English Folk Song

TRACK 1 • 42

2.10 JINGLE BELLS – Duet

James S. Pierpont

TRACK 1 • 43

BB208OB

13a

ON THE PODIUM

When dynamics indicate *loud*, a conductor's gestures are bigger.

When dynamics indicate *soft*, gestures are smaller.

Practice conducting a four-beat pattern with dynamics!

2.11 DREIDEL SONG

Traditional Hannukah Song

THEORY

DYNAMICS

Mezzo is an Italian term that means "medium" or "moderately." The letter *m* is an abbreviation used in dynamics.

mp (*mezzo piano*) – play moderately soft   *mf* (*mezzo forte*) – play moderately loud

2.12 BEAT STREET *Clap the dynamics!*

CLAP

2.13 DYNAMIC DOODLE ALL DAY

American Folk Melody

THEORY

PICK-UP NOTES

Pick-up notes lead into the first full measure of a phrase.

When pick-up notes are used to begin a piece, their combined rhythmic value is often subtracted from the last measure.

2.14 A–TISKET, A–TASKET

American Folk Song

2.15 OH! SUSANNA – Duet

Stephen C. Foster

13b

When dynamics indicate *loud*, a conductor's gestures are bigger.
When dynamics indicate *soft*, gestures are smaller.
Practice conducting a four-beat pattern with dynamics!

2.11 DREIDEL SONG

Traditional Hannukah Song — TRACK 1 44

DYNAMICS

Mezzo is an Italian term that means "medium" or "moderately." The letter *m* is an abbreviation used in dynamics.

mp (*mezzo piano*) – play moderately soft   *mf* (*mezzo forte*) – play moderately loud

2.12 BEAT STREET *Clap the dynamics!*

TRACK 1 45

2.13 DYNAMIC DOODLE ALL DAY

American Folk Melody — TRACK 1 46

PICK-UP NOTES

Pick-up notes lead into the first full measure of a phrase.
When pick-up notes are used to begin a piece, their combined rhythmic value is often subtracted from the last measure.

2.14 A–TISKET, A–TASKET

American Folk Song — TRACK 1 47

2.15 OH! SUSANNA – Duet

Stephen C. Foster — TRACK 1 48

BB208OB

14a

2.16 AFRICAN SAFARI

ARTICULATION: ACCENT

> An **accent** indicates to emphasize a note by playing louder. Use your air!

2.17 LEAN ON IT

2.18 WALK TO MY LOU

American Folk Melody

SYNCOPATION

Music has strong beats and weak beats. Most of the time, we stress strong beats (**1** 2 **3** 4).
Sometimes, we shift the stress onto weak beats (1 **2** 3 **4**).
This is known as **syncopation**. Longer, accented notes that occur on weak beats often identify syncopation.

2.19 BEAT STREET

2.20 SHOO FLY

American Folk Song

2.20A FORK IT OVER – OBOES ONLY *Oboes use the forked F fingering when leaving or approaching E♭ or D.*

American Folk Song

2.21 CHANT

use forked F *throughout*

2.16 AFRICAN SAFARI

TRACK 1 49

THEORY

ARTICULATION: ACCENT

> An **accent** indicates to emphasize a note by playing louder. Use your air!

2.17 LEAN ON IT

TRACK 1 50

2.18 WALK TO MY LOU

American Folk Melody

TRACK 1 51

RHYTHM 13 2/4

SYNCOPATION

Music has strong beats and weak beats. Most of the time, we stress strong beats (**1** 2 **3** 4).
Sometimes, we shift the stress onto weak beats (1 **2** 3 **4**).
This is known as **syncopation**. Longer, accented notes that occur on weak beats often identify syncopation.

2.19 BEAT STREET

TRACK 1 52

CLAP

2.20 SHOO FLY

American Folk Song

TRACK 1 53

2.21 CHANT

TRACK 1 54

14c

RANGE STUDIES — OBOE ONLY

A PAGES

If you have been playing from the left side of the book (A pages), these exercises will teach you the new notes and key signature you need to know in order to play the rest of the book.

B PAGES

If you have been playing from the right side of the book (B pages), these exercises will reinforce the notes you have learned.

2.21A CLIMBING THE LADDER

NEW NOTE! E♭

2.21B SIMPLE GIFTS *Use the forked F fingering when leaving or approaching E♭.*

Joseph Brackett, Jr.

NEW NOTE! FORKED F

THEORY

NEW KEY SIGNATURE

This is the key of B♭ Major.

This key signature indicates that all Bs should be played as B-flats and all Es should be played as E-flats.

2.21C ANGELS WE HAVE HEARD ON HIGH *Also use forked F when leaving or approaching D.*

French Carol

use forked F *throughout*

2.21D ERIE CANAL

American Folk Song

NEW NOTE! G

2.21E CAN CAN

Jacques Offenbach

2.21F FINAL ASCENT

2.21G ROCKY MOUNTAIN

Southern Folk Song

OPUS 2 ENCORE!

INTERPRETATION STATION

Listen to CD 1 Track 55. You will hear two performances of the same piece. Which one is more musical and why?

SIMON "SEZ"

Listen to CD 1 Track 56. You will hear a well-known song. Listen first, sing it, then find the pitches on your instrument. You can then play along with the accompaniment track that follows. Can you match the initial recording?

COMPOSER'S CORNER

Use the notes and rhythms you have learned to complete the composition. Be sure to give it a title!

Title:_____ Name:_____

PENCIL POWER

The Secret Decoder: Name the notes and solve the puzzles!

1.

Beethoven went ___ ___ ___ ___ towards the end of his life.

2.

The ___ ___ ___ ___ in the ___ ___ ___ ___ photo h___ ___ ___ ___ ___ with time.

3.

H___ h___ ___ to pay an extra ___ ___ ___ for the ___ i ___ ___ ___ ___ ___ .

4.

He ___ ___ ___ ___ ___ when he mistakenly ate ___ ___ ___ corned ___ ___ ___ and ___ ___ ___ ___ !

CURTAIN UP!

2.22 TOKECANG
Traditional Indonesian

BB208OB

CURTAIN UP!

2.28 FANFARE FOR A WINTER CELEBRATION – Full Band

arr. Brian Balmages

TRACK 1 63

2.29 THE SECTION BATTLE RAG – Full Band

Brian Balmages

TRACK 1 64

16 **Section Feature!**
Circle the measure(s) your director asks you to play! - - - - - - - - - - - - - - - - tutti (everyone)

2.30 ON CARIBBEAN SHORES (MARY ANN) – Full Band

Jamaican Folk Song
arr. Robert Sheldon

TRACK 1 65

2.31 ROCK THE HOUSE – Full Band

Brian Balmages

TRACK 1 66

BB208OB

✳ OPUS 3

MORE TIME SIGNATURES

RHYTHM
13
2⁴

3/4   **3 beats** in each measure
Quarter note gets one beat

2/4   **2 beats** in each measure
Quarter note gets one beat

3.1 BEAT STREET
CLAP
TRACK 1 67

3.2 THREE'S A CROWD
TRACK 1 68

3.3 THREE POINTER
TRACK 1 69

3.4 BEAT STREET
CLAP
TRACK 1 70

3.5 RAIN, RAIN, GO AWAY
Traditional
TRACK 1 71

ON THE PODIUM

CONDUCTING IN 2/4 TIME

It is your turn to conduct a two-beat pattern.
With your right hand in a "handshake" position,
follow the diagram to conduct in 2/4 time.

3.6 TWO FOR YOU
ON THE PODIUM
TRACK 1 72

3.7 TERRIBLE TWOS
TRACK 1 73

REVISITING ACCIDENTALS

Accidentals include **flat** (♭), **sharp** (♯), and **natural** (♮) signs found in front of notes, but not in the key signature.
A flat sign (♭) lowers the pitch one half-step. It remains in effect for the rest of the measure.

3.8 CANYONS

NEW KEY SIGNATURE

This is the key of E♭ **Major.**

This key signature indicates that all Bs, Es, and As should be played as B-flats, E-flats, and A-flats.

3.9 ROYAL SCEPTER *Musicianship Challenge! – Play this piece in a noble style.*

3.10 THINGS ARE LOOKING UP *Add a breath mark after the first phrase.*

THE RULE OF THE DOT

Adding a dot after a note increases the length of the note *by half its value.*
When adding a dot to a half note, it becomes a **dotted half note.**

2 beats + 1 beat = 3 beats   2 beats + 1 beat = 3 beats

3.11 BEAT STREET

Begin CD 2

3.12 TRIPLE CROWN

3.13 MINUET

Daniel G. Türk

BB208OB

21

3.21 SKIP TO MY LOU

American Folk Song — TRACK 2 · 11

 RHYTHM

WHOLE MEASURE REST

 Rest for the entire measure. Check the time signature!

3.22 WALTZING LOU *How should you play these dynamics?*

American Folk Melody — TRACK 2 · 12

(1 - 2 - 3)

THEORY

ENCLOSED REPEAT SIGNS

Repeat the music between the two signs.

3.23 TWO BY FOUR

TRACK 2 · 13

THEORY

STYLE AND FORM: ROUND

In a **round**, each musician plays the same part, but enters at a different time.

3.24 FRÉRE JACQUES – Round *As each musician reaches ②, the next musician should begin playing at ①.*

French Folk Song — TRACK 2 · 14

THEORY

STYLE AND FORM: THEME AND VARIATIONS

Composers create a **variation** when they change a melody in some way. Changes can be made to the notes, rhythm, key, and even the time signature! While you will notice the differences in each variation, you will still be able to recognize the original theme.

A **double bar line** indicates the end of one section and the beginning of another.

3.25 VARIATIONS ON A FRENCH MELODY

TRACK 2 · 15

BB208OB

THEORY

DYNAMICS

Crescendo means to gradually play louder.   **Decrescendo** means to gradually play softer.

3.26 IT'S SWELL *Clap first, then play!*
TRACK 2 16

3.27 OUTTA MY WAY
TRACK 2 17

3.28 REGAL FANFARE
TRACK 2 18

NEW NOTE! F

regular F

HISTORY

MUSIC
German born **George Frideric Handel** (1685 – 1759) composed many types of music including oratorios, operas, and orchestral works. *Music for the Royal Fireworks* was written when George II of Great Britain hired him to write music to accompany fireworks in London. The event commemorated the signing of the Treaty of Aix-la-Chapelle in 1749.

ART
During colonial times, American painting and drawing focused on portraiture. Joseph Badger painted portraits of prominent figures and children in colonial Boston. His style can be seen in the portrait of *Jeremiah Belknap*, painted in 1758.

WORLD
Sir Isaac Newton stated the three universal laws of motion. In the same publication he used the Latin word *gravitas* that would become known as gravity. Also, America founded its first hospital in Pennsylvania.

3.29 MUSIC FOR THE ROYAL FIREWORKS
George F. Handel   TRACK 2 19

regular

forked

RHYTHM 13 4 / 2 4

BEAM GROUPS

3.30 SCALE THE WALL
TRACK 2 20

23

BB208OB

OPUS 3 ENCORE!

INTERPRETATION STATION

TRACK 2 26

Listen to CD 2 Track 26. You will hear four musical examples, all composed using a different time signature.
As you listen, pay close attention to how rhythmic ideas are grouped. Circle the correct time signature for each example.

1. $\frac{3}{4}$ $\frac{4}{4}$ 2. $\frac{2}{4}$ $\frac{3}{4}$ 3. $\frac{3}{4}$ $\frac{4}{4}$ 4. $\frac{2}{4}$ $\frac{3}{4}$

SIMON "SEZ"

TRACK 2 27

Listen to CD 2 Track 27. You are going to hear a piece called *One Note Wonder.* It gets its title because it uses only one pitch!
You will hear dynamics that make it very interesting. Play along with the accompaniment track that follows, imitating the dynamics
and rhythm of the initial recording to make it musical.

COMPOSER'S CORNER

It is your turn to be a composer again! Use notes and rhythms you have learned to complete each measure (remember to
look at the time signature). Then give your piece a title and perform it for a friend or family member!

Title:_____   Name:_____

PENCIL POWER

Each measure below is rhythmically incomplete! For each example, add *one note* to complete the measure and make it correct.

CURTAIN UP!

3.36 ZUM GALI GALI – Round

Traditional Hebrew Song

TRACK 2 28

3.37 DRY BONES

Spiritual

TRACK 2 29

MULTIPLE MEASURE REST

In some pieces, there will be instances when you rest for a few measures at a time. When this happens, you will see the **multiple measure rest** symbol. The number above the symbol tells you how many measures of rest to count.

Count: **1** 2 3 4 | **2** 2 3 4

This symbol tells you to rest for two measures in $\frac{4}{4}$ time.

1 2 3 | **2** 2 3 | **3** 2 3

This symbol tells you to rest for three measures in $\frac{3}{4}$ time.

3.38 WILLIAM TELL OVERTURE

Gioachino Rossini
arr. Brian Balmages

3.39 ABOVE THE CLOUDS

Robert Sheldon

✳ OPUS 4

4.0 REGULAR OR DECAF? – FOR OBOES ONLY

NEW NOTE! F

regular F

4.1 CIRCUS ACT *Use regular F throughout.*

NEW NOTE! E

TRACK **2** 32

mf

E

f

4.2 DAYBREAK

TRACK **2** 33

ON THE PODIUM

Legato *(smooth and flowing)*

mp

THEORY

NEW KEY SIGNATURE

This is the key of **F Major**

This key signature indicates that all Bs should be played as B-flats.

4.3 CHIAPANECAS

TRACK **2** 34

Mexican Folk Song

BONUS BOX

new key signature

mf

stomp

THEORY

ARTICULATION: SLUR

A **slur** is a curved line that connects notes of *different* pitches. Tongue only the first note of a slur.

4.4 SLURRED NOT SHAKEN

TRACK **2** 35

NEW NOTE! A

Legato

A

mp

4.5 SLIP 'N' SLIDE

TRACK **2** 36

p

mf

p

27

TEMPO

Tempo is the speed of the beat. Music can move at different rates of speed.

Largo – a slow tempo   **Moderato** – a medium tempo   **Allegro** – a fast tempo

4.6 MUSETTE

J.S. Bach

Moderato

4.7 CIELITO LINDO

Mexican Folk Song

Allegro

HISTORY

MUSIC

Gustav Mahler (1860 – 1911) was a noted composer and conductor of the late Romantic era. He spent time in New York conducting the Metropolitan Opera and the New York Philharmonic Orchestra. He is mainly known for his large symphonies (his *Symphony No. 8* uses over a thousand performers!).

ART

The world saw the emergence of Cubism, a style in which objects were broken up, then reassembled in abstract forms. Pablo Picasso became one of the most famous Cubists in history. His *Ma Jolie* (1911) is an early example of the style.

WORLD

Mark Twain published *The Adventures of Tom Sawyer*, Sir Arthur Conan Doyle introduced the world to Sherlock Holmes, and the coin-operated telephone was invented.

4.8 THEME FROM SYMPHONY NO. 1 – Round

Gustav Mahler

Largo

RHYTHM

TIE

A **tie** is a curved line that connects notes of the *same* pitch. These notes are "tied" together and played to sound like one longer note.

4.9 MAKING CONNECTIONS

4.10 ALL TIED UP

BB208OB

HISTORY

MUSIC

Pyotr Ilyich Tchaikovsky (1840 – 1893) was a Russian composer who studied music at a very young age. His most famous works include the ballet *The Nutcracker* and the exciting *1812 Overture*. He composed *Capriccio Italien* after a visit to Italy during Carnivale season.

ART

In 1880, the Arts and Crafts Movement was going strong in England. This style is reflected in art, architecture, and interior design. Works by British architect Herbert Tudor Buckland and American architect Frank Lloyd Wright are typical of the Arts and Crafts style.

WORLD

Wabash, Indiana became the first town to be completely illuminated using electric light and the Statue of Liberty was presented to the United States by the people of France.

4.11 CAPRICCIO ITALIEN *How many slurs are in this piece?*

Pyotr I. Tchaikovsky — TRACK 2 42

4.12 BARCAROLLE

Jacques Offenbach — TRACK 2 43

NEW NOTE! **D♭**

THEORY

NEW KEY SIGNATURE

This is the key of A♭ Major.

This key signature indicates that all Bs, Es, As, and Ds should be played as B-flats, E-flats, A-flats, and D-flats.

4.13 THE BLUE BELLS OF SCOTLAND

Scottish Folk Song — TRACK 2 44

HISTORY

MUSIC

John Philip Sousa (1854 – 1932) was a violinist, composer, and conductor born in Washington, D.C. He conducted the United States Marine Band from 1880 until 1892. His marches, such as *The Stars and Stripes Forever, Semper Fidelis*, and the *Liberty Bell*, are well known and important to American culture.

ART

In the early 20th century, artist Salvador Dali of Spain was mostly known as a surrealist and emphasized visions of the subconscious. *The Persistence of Memory* (1931), a scene with melting clocks, is one of his best known works.

WORLD

Elsewhere in 1917, the Russian revolution began, World War I was still raging, and the first commercial recordings of jazz music were available to the public.

4.14 HIGH SCHOOL CADETS

John Philip Sousa — TRACK 2 45

4.15 IT'S ONLY NATURAL

4.16 ACCIDENTAL BLUES – Duet

courtesy accidental

RETURN OF THE DOT RULE

Adding a dot after a note increases the length of the note by half its value. Here, the dot is used with a quarter note to create a **dotted quarter note**.

4.17 BEAT STREET *Tap your foot to keep a steady beat.*

4.18 DOTS A LOT

RITARDANDO

Ritardando – abbreviated "*rit.*" – means to make the tempo gradually slower.

4.19 ALL THROUGH THE NIGHT

Welsh Folk Song

BB208OB

4.20 AMERICA

Maestoso

Traditional

D.C. AL FINE

D.C. is an abbreviation for *da capo*, an Italian term that refers to the beginning.
At the **D.C. al Fine**, return to the beginning and play again until the **Fine**.

4.21 ALOUETTE

Moderato

French-Canadian Folk Song

4.22 BANANA BOAT SONG *Calypso is a blend of African and Caribbean music.*

Calypso

Caribbean Folk Song

MUSIC

Antonín Dvořák (1841 – 1904) was from a small town near Prague, in the Czech Republic. He eventually moved to the United States and became the director of the New York Conservatory of Music. In 1888, the Conservatory welcomed African-Americans while other schools were still practicing segregation. His *Symphony No. 9 ("From the New World")* was composed during his brief time in America. It is influenced by Native American music and African-American spirituals.

ART

French artist Georges Seurat painted *A Sunday Afternoon on the Island of La Grande Jatte*. This large painting, depicting a scene of recreation in Paris, was created using a technique called pointillism. Composed entirely of painted dots, it took him nearly two years to finish.

WORLD

Congress abolished slavery in the U.S. Territories, Albert Einstein was born, the World's Columbian Exposition was held in Chicago, and New York became the first state to require license plates on cars.

4.23 THEME FROM THE NEW WORLD SYMPHONY

Largo

Antonín Dvořák

MORE ABOUT THE DOT

While a dotted quarter note is usually followed by an eighth note,
the eighth note sometimes appears *before* the dotted quarter note.

4.24 BEAT STREET

4.25 CARIBBEAN CARNIVAL

4.26 GOOD NIGHT LADIES

Traditional

4.27 GOING TO KENTUCKY

American Folk Song

4.28 FILL 'ER UP *A deep breath and full airstream will help you play with a beautiful sound.*

4.29 MARCHE MILITAIRE

Franz Schubert

OPUS 4 ENCORE!

INTERPRETATION STATION

TRACK 2 / 61

Listen to CD 2 Track 61. For each example, decide if the tempo is **Largo**, **Moderato**, or **Allegro**.
Circle the correct answer.

1. L M A   2. L M A   3. L M A   4. L M A

SIMON "SEZ"

TRACK 2 / 62

Listen to CD 2 Track 62. You are going to hear the same five-note pattern articulated four different ways.
Match the performance to its correctly notated example. The first one has been done for you!

No. 1 = __B__   No. 2 = _____   No. 3 = _____   No. 4 = _____

COMPOSER'S CORNER

Sometimes a composer takes an existing melody and presents it in a new way. This is called **arranging**. Change the rhythms of the music in
Alouette in Four so it is playable in $\frac{2}{4}$ time. *Hint: Cut the rhythmic value of each note in half!* The arrangement has been started for you.

ALOUETTE IN FOUR

ALOUETTE IN TWO

PENCIL POWER – MATCH THE COMPOSER

Match the composer with the correct fact by writing in the appropriate letter.

_____ Wolfgang Amadeus Mozart   A. Russian composer who wrote the famous ballet, *The Nutcracker*

_____ Antonín Dvořák   B. U.S. Marine Band conductor and composer known for his marches

_____ Gustav Mahler   C. His *Symphony No. 9* reveals the influence of African-American spirituals

_____ John Philip Sousa   D. Child genius who composed over 600 works in a short life of 35 years

_____ Ludwig van Beethoven   E. Continued to compose music after becoming completely deaf

_____ Pyotr Ilyich Tchaikovsky   F. Composer of the late Romantic era known for his large symphonies

CURTAIN UP!

4.30 HAVA NASHIRA – Round

Israeli Folk Song   **TRACK 2 / 63**

CURTAIN UP!

4.31 LITTLE SWALLOW *divisi (div.) – Part of the section plays the top note and part of the section plays the bottom note.*

Chinese Folk Song
arr. Robert Sheldon

4.32 FURY

Brian Balmages

BB208OB

34

4.33 HAIL THE CONQUERING HERO
Instrumental Solo

George F. Handel
arr. Brian Balmages

Piano Accompaniment

✴ OPUS 5

In this Opus, focus on breath support and sound. Strive to hold all notes for their full value, especially those connected by a slur or tie.

5.1 CATAPULT!

Begin CD 3

TRACK 3 1

5.2 UP AND OVER

TRACK 3 2

5.3 SMOOTH HORIZONS

TRACK 3 3

5.4 UP, UP AND AWAY!

TRACK 3 4

5.5 CLIMB ON

TRACK 3 5

5.6 OVER EASY

TRACK 3 6

5.7 ZERO GRAVITY

TRACK 3 7

5.8 BREAKING THROUGH

TRACK 3 8

5.9 THE MOON TURNS DARK

Misterioso *(mysteriously)*

French Folk Melody

TRACK 3 9

BB208OB

5.10 IN ORBIT

5.11 CLEAR SKIES

5.12 SPIRIT!

Marziale

5.13 BREAK IT DOWN

5.14 SHALOM, CHAVERIM

Allegro

Hebrew Folk Song

1.

2.

5.15 THE UNDISCOVERED PLANET

Aggressively

THEORY

TEMPO

Andante is a tempo between *Largo* and *Moderato*.

slow ⟷ fast

Largo – Andante – Moderato – Allegro

5.16 SAKURA, SAKURA

Andante

Japanese Folk Song

37

HISTORY

MUSIC

German composer **Johannes Brahms** (1833 – 1897) was also an accomplished pianist and gave the first performance of many of his own works. *Lullaby (Wiegenlied)* was composed in 1868 to celebrate the birth of his friend's son.

ART

In the mid 1800s, Realists were concerned with objectivity. American artist James Whistler titled many of his works "harmonies" or "arrangements." An example is his *Arrangement in Grey and Black No. 1: Portrait of the Artist's Mother.*

WORLD

In 1868, floats appeared in New Orleans' Mardi Gras parade for the first time and the first Memorial Day was celebrated in the United States.

5.17 LULLABY – Duet

Johannes Brahms

Cantabile *(in a singing style)*

EIGHTH RESTS

The **eighth rest** receives one-half beat in $\frac{4}{4}$ time.

Eighth rests can replace upbeat eighth notes.

Eighth rests can replace downbeat eighth notes.

5.18 BEAT STREET

5.19 SCALING WITH EIGHTH RESTS

HISTORY

MUSIC

German composer **Johann Sebastian Bach** (1685 – 1750) began learning music as a young boy, studying violin and organ. He is thought to be one of the greatest composers who ever lived. His work is the model of the Baroque style.

ART

Peter Paul Rubens painted a series of works in the Baroque Style for Marie de Medici at the Luxembourg Palace in Paris, France. These works are now on display at the Louvre, one of the most famous art museums in the world.

WORLD

The tuning fork was invented by Englishman John Shore, the first folding umbrella was manufactured in France, and infamous pirate Edward Teach (Blackbeard) terrorized people along the Atlantic coast.

5.20 MINUET NO. 1

J. S. Bach

Moderato

BB208OB

38

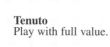

ARTICULATION: TENUTO AND STACCATO

Tenuto
Play with full value.

Staccato
Play light and separated.

5.25 LONG AND SHORT OF IT

TRACK 3 25

HISTORY

MUSIC
Austrian composer **Franz Joseph Haydn** (1732 – 1809) is often referred to as the father of the symphony (He wrote 108 of them!). *Symphony No. 94* is often called the *Surprise Symphony*. Haydn surprised listeners with an unexpected loud chord that came after some very quiet music.

ART
Americans saw paintings by countryman John Trumbull (his historical painting *Declaration of Independence* is on the back of the $2 bill). In England, young artist Joseph Turner was setting the tone for Impressionism.

WORLD
The United States Bill of Rights was ratified, the world's first Sunday newspaper (*The Observer*) was published in England, and Benjamin Franklin invented bifocals!

5.26 SURPRISE SYMPHONY

Franz J. Haydn

TRACK 3 26

Andante

HISTORY

MUSIC
Paul Abraham Dukas (1865 – 1935) was a French composer who wrote in the Romantic style. His most famous work, *The Sorcerer's Apprentice,* is based on a poem by Johann Wolfgang von Goethe. The poem describes an apprentice who loses control of an enchanted broomstick.

ART
Edvard Munch, from Norway, painted in the Expressionist style which uses symbolism to portray many different themes. One of his best-known works is *The Scream* (1893).

WORLD
The 19th Amendment gave women the right to vote, author Madeleine L'Engle was born, and the first underground metro railway opened in Boston.

5.27 THE SORCERER'S APPRENTICE

Paul A. Dukas

TRACK 3 27

Misterioso

5.28 GO DOWN MOSES

Spiritual

TRACK 3 28

NEW NOTE!
G♭

5.29 JITTERS, CRITTERS

TRACK 3 29

Misterioso

BB208OB

OPUS 5 ENCORE!

INTERPRETATION STATION

Listen to CD 3 Track 30. For each example, decide if the articulation is *Legato* or *Staccato*.
Circle the letter that corresponds with your answer.

1. L S   2. L S   3. L S   4. L S

SIMON "SEZ"

Listen to CD 3 Track 31. You will hear a well-known song. Listen first, sing it, then find the pitches on your instrument. You can then play along with the accompaniment track that follows. Can you match the notes and style of the initial recording?

COMPOSER'S CORNER

Writing a theme is just one part of a composer's process. Composers also use dynamics to make their music more expressive.
Add your own dynamics and then play the piece expressively. Choose from the following:

PENCIL POWER – MATCH THE STYLE TERMS

Match the style term with the correct definition by writing in the appropriate letter.

_____ Legato		A.	In a singing style
_____ Maestoso		B.	In a march style
_____ Dolce		C.	Smooth and flowing
_____ Marziale		D.	Sweetly
_____ Cantabile		E.	Blend of African and Caribbean music
_____ Calypso		F.	Majestically

CURTAIN UP!

5.30 LOCH LOMOND

Scottish Folk Song

5.31 LA MORISQUE (RENAISSANCE DANCE)

Tielman Susato
arr. Brian Balmages

TRACK 3 33

5.32 COSSACK'S MARCHING SONG

Russian Folk Song
arr. Robert Sheldon

TRACK 3 34

✸ OPUS 6

ENHARMONICS

Two notes that have the same pitch but different names are called **enharmonics**. An example would be G♭ and F♯.
They have different names but share the same fingering and sound the same when played!

43

HISTORY

MUSIC

Italian born **Giuseppe Verdi** (1813 – 1901) is best known for his operas, especially *Il Trovatore* (The Troubadour), first performed in 1853. The *Anvil Chorus*, from Act 2 of *Il Trovatore*, features Spanish gypsies who sing and strike anvils as they work in the early morning.

ART

Art in the style of Luminism began in the 1850s and was characterized by the use of light effects best seen in sea and landscapes. This American style is found in works by Frederic Church (*Twilight in the Wilderness*) and Martin Heade (*Sunlight and Shadow: The Newbury Marshes*).

WORLD

In 1853, when *Il Trovatore* premiered, the Ottoman Empire declared war on Russia, the Gadsden Purchase (currently southern Arizona and New Mexico) was made, and potato chips made their first tasty appearance.

6.7 ANVIL CHORUS

Pesante *(heavily)*

Giuseppe Verdi

THEORY

MORE DYNAMICS

cresc. — Sometimes this abbreviation is used in place of a crescendo sign. It means the same thing as the sign; gradually play louder.

decresc. — Sometimes this abbreviation is used in place of a decrescendo sign. It means the same thing as the sign; gradually play softer.

6.8 YANKEE DOODLE CAME AND WENT

Moderato

American Folk Melody

THEORY

MAJOR SCALE, ARPEGGIO, AND CHORD

A **major scale** has eight notes going up or down in consecutive order, all in the key signature of the scale name. In your key of B♭ Major, all eight notes are in the key signature of B♭ Major, which has 2 flats. The top and bottom notes are both B♭. The distance between these notes is called an **octave**.

An **arpeggio** is the first, third, and fifth notes of a scale played in *succession*. It may also include the 8th scale note.

A **major chord** is the first, third, and fifth notes of a major scale played *simultaneously*. Like the arpeggio, it may also include the 8th scale note.

6.9 CONCERT B♭ MAJOR SCALE

6.10 CONCERT B♭ MAJOR ARPEGGIO AND CHORD

BB208OB

44

6.11 KUM BAH YAH *Circle the arpeggios.*

African Folk Song

mp   *pp*

mp   *cresc.*   *mf*   *decresc.*   *pp*

INTERVALS

An **interval** is the distance between two pitches. You can figure out the interval by counting each line and space between the notes. Starting with "1" on the bottom note, count upward until you reach the top note. The number of the top note identifies the interval.

unison   2nd   3rd   4th   5th   6th   7th   octave

6.12 RANGE ROVER *Identify each interval, counting from the bottom note.*

ON THE PODIUM

6.13 HATIKVAH

Israeli National Anthem

Andante

mp

6

mf

14   *rit.*

f

6.14 HEY!

ON THE PODIUM

Allegro

f

Hey!

BB208OB

MORE ABOUT SYNCOPATION

You already know the quarter-half-quarter syncopation. The most common syncopated rhythm is eighth-quarter-eighth. Here the syncopation occurs on the accented upbeat quarter note.

6.15 BEAT STREET

6.16 SYNCOPHOBIA

6.17 THE CAISSONS GO ROLLING ALONG

6.18 LI'L LIZA JANE

6.19 MAYIM, MAYIM – Duet
An ostinato is a musical pattern that is repeated over and over again. It is typically based on a short melodic or rhythmic idea and is generally performed by the same instrument part.

6.20 COVENTRY CAROL

BB208OB

46

6.21 DIES IRAE

att. Thomas of Celano

TRACK 3 55

Pesante

6.22 LEAGUE OF SUPERHEROES

TRACK 3 56

Allegro

THEORY

CHROMATIC SCALE

A **half step** is the smallest interval between two pitches. Two consecutive half steps make a **whole step**. The **chromatic scale** has thirteen notes going up and down in consecutive half steps.

6.23 CHROMATIC SCALE

TRACK 3 57

no key signature!   *half step*   *whole step*

HISTORY

MUSIC

Georges Bizet (1838 – 1875) was a child prodigy from Paris who composed his first symphony in 1855 when he was just 16! In his short 36-year life, he wrote many different types of music but is best known for his operas. His most famous opera is *Carmen*.

ART

The Impressionistic style was all the rage in the art world. Edgar Degas had painted *In Concert Cafe*, *The Song of the Dog*. American realist painter Thomas Eakins completed the *Gross Clinic*, a very real rendition of a surgeon overseeing an operation to remove part of a diseased thighbone.

WORLD

Events in 1875 included the first organized indoor ice hockey game in Montreal, the running of the first Kentucky Derby, and the patent of the electric dental drill.

6.24 HABAÑERA (FROM CARMEN) – Duet *Where is the ostinato?*

Georges Bizet

TRACK 3 58

Moderato

BB208OB

OPUS 6 ENCORE!

INTERPRETATION STATION

TRACK 3 59

Listen to CD 3 Track 59. For each musical example, decide if the melody is based on a <u>Scale</u> or an <u>Arpeggio</u>.
Circle the letter that corresponds with your answer.

1. S A   2. S A   3. S A   4. S A

SIMON "SEZ"

TRACK 3 60

Listen to CD 3 Track 60. You will hear a well-known piece. Listen first, sing it, then find the pitches on your instrument.
You can then play along with the accompaniment track that follows. Can you match the notes and style of the initial recording?

COMPOSER'S CORNER

Performers sometimes compose music on the spot while they are playing! This is called **improvisation.** There is an ostinato below.
Have a partner play it (or use CD 3 Track 61 as a background track) while you improvise. Use the guide notes to help you out. Have fun!
Note: The CD recording repeats 4 times.

"WHATEVER!"

TRACK 3 61

PENCIL POWER

On the staff below, notate the enharmonic for each note. See if you can figure out the bonus notes!

CURTAIN UP!

6.25 O CANADA

Canadian National Anthem
Calixa Lavallée, Sir Adolphe-Basile Routhier, and Justice R.S. Weir

TRACK 3 62

BB208OB

48

CURTAIN UP! FULL BAND

6.26 CHORALE IN B♭ MAJOR
(ALLE MENSCHEN MÜSSEN STERBEN)

J. S. Bach

TRACK 3 63

Andante

6.27 RABBLE ROUSER

Robert Sheldon

TRACK 3 64

Allegro

6.28 PROCESSION OF THE CHAMPIONS

Brian Balmages

TRACK **3** 65

Andante

BB208OB

50

6.29 ROYAL MARCH OF THE LION
Instrumental Solo

Camille Saint-Saëns
arr. Brian Balmages

TRACK 3 66

Piano Accompaniment

Note: Sections are repeated in the accompaniment for spacing reasons and do not always follow the solo part.

TRACK 3 67

(Piano accompaniment only)

BB208OB

SCALES AND TECHNIQUE

CONCERT B♭ MAJOR

SCALE

SCALE IN THIRDS

CONCERT E♭ MAJOR

SCALE

SCALE IN THIRDS

CONCERT A♭ MAJOR

SCALE

SCALE IN THIRDS

CONCERT F MAJOR

SCALE

SCALE IN THIRDS

CHROMATIC SCALE

RHYTHM REVIEW – OPUS 1-6

OBOE KEY LAYOUT

h.h.

PRACTICING TIPS

Some exercises will be very easy for you to master while others will require more diligent practice. Be prepared to spend more time on the music that is difficult for you. Above all, be consistent in your approach and always end with something fun! The enclosed CDs are a great tool to help you practice, but it is important that you also practice alone.

- Find a **quiet place** where you can practice without distraction.
- Practice at the **same time each day** so it becomes part of your daily schedule.
- Use a **straight back chair** and a **music stand** to promote good posture.
- Begin with a **regular warm-up routine**.
- Practice your **lesson assignments** and **band music**, spending additional time on challenging sections.
- Wrap up your practice by playing **something fun**!

Photograph courtesy of Yamaha Corporation of America

OBOE FINGERING CHART

○ = open

● = pressed down

h.h. = half hole

Sometimes it is better to use an alternate fingering to make technique smoother. These alternate fingerings are displayed after the more common fingerings.

INDEX